inspirational Filet Crochet

Let filet crochet tell the world what's important to you. Unique borders surround eight thought-provoking words, emphasizing the message of each one. Declare your affection with *BELOVED*, *CHERISH*, or *PRECIOUS*. Share inspiration with *BELIEVE*, *COURAGE*, *PROMISE*, and *STRENGTH*. Or extend hospitality with *WELCOME*. The designs are perfect for framed wall décor and are lovely when topping a pillow. Clearly charted for you to fashion with bedspread cotton in your choice of size 10, 20, or 30 (we used size 10 for the photo models), these lacy creations are sure to bless your heart and your home for many years to come. And just imagine what meaningful gifts they would make!

LEISURE ARTS, INC.
Maumelle, AR

Lattice *Believe*

EASY

Finished Size:
Size 10: 38"w x 15"h (96.5 cm x 38 cm)
Size 20: 33 3/4"w x 13 1/2"h (85.5 cm x 34.5 cm)
Size 30: 30 1/2"w x 12 1/4"h (77.5 cm x 31 cm)

Size Note: Materials, gauge, and gauge swatch are written for cotton thread size 10, with sizes 20 and 30 in braces { }. If only one number is given, it applies to all three weights of thread.

MATERIALS
Cotton Thread
Size 10 - [400 yards (365 meters) per ball]: 3 balls
Size 20 - [400 yards (365 meters) per ball]: 3 balls
Size 30 - [500 yards (457 meters) per ball]: 3 balls
Steel crochet hook, size 6{8-10}/1.8{1.5-1.3} mm **or** size needed for gauge

GAUGE: 18{20-22} dc and 8{9-10} rows = 2" (5 cm)

Gauge Swatch: 2" (5 cm) square
Ch 20{22-24}.
Row 1: Dc in fourth ch from hook **(3 skipped chs count as first dc)** and in each ch across: 18{20-22} dc.
Rows 2 thru 8{9-10}: Ch 3 **(counts as first dc)**, turn; dc in next dc and in each dc across.
Finish off.

BASIC CHART STITCHES

BEGINNING BLOCK OVER BLOCK
Ch 3 **(counts as first dc, now and throughout)**, turn; dc in next 3 dc.
BLOCK OVER BLOCK
Dc in next 3 dc.
BLOCK OVER SPACE
2 Dc in next ch-2 sp, dc in next dc.
SPACE OVER BLOCK
Ch 2, skip next 2 dc, dc in next dc.
SPACE OVER SPACE
Ch 2, dc in next dc.

INSTRUCTIONS

Ch 138.

Row 1: Dc in fourth ch from hook **(3 skipped chs count as first dc)** and in each ch across: 136 dc.

Row 2 (Right side)**:** Work Beginning Block, work Blocks across: 45 Blocks.

Note: Loop a short piece of thread around any stitch to mark Row 2 as **right** side.

Rows 3-6: Work Beginning Block, work 3 Spaces, work Block, ★ (work Space, work Block) twice, work 3 Spaces, work Block; repeat from ★ across.

Rows 7-152: Follow Charts, pages 4 and 5.

Finish off.

See Washing and Blocking, page 35.

BELIEVE

CHART

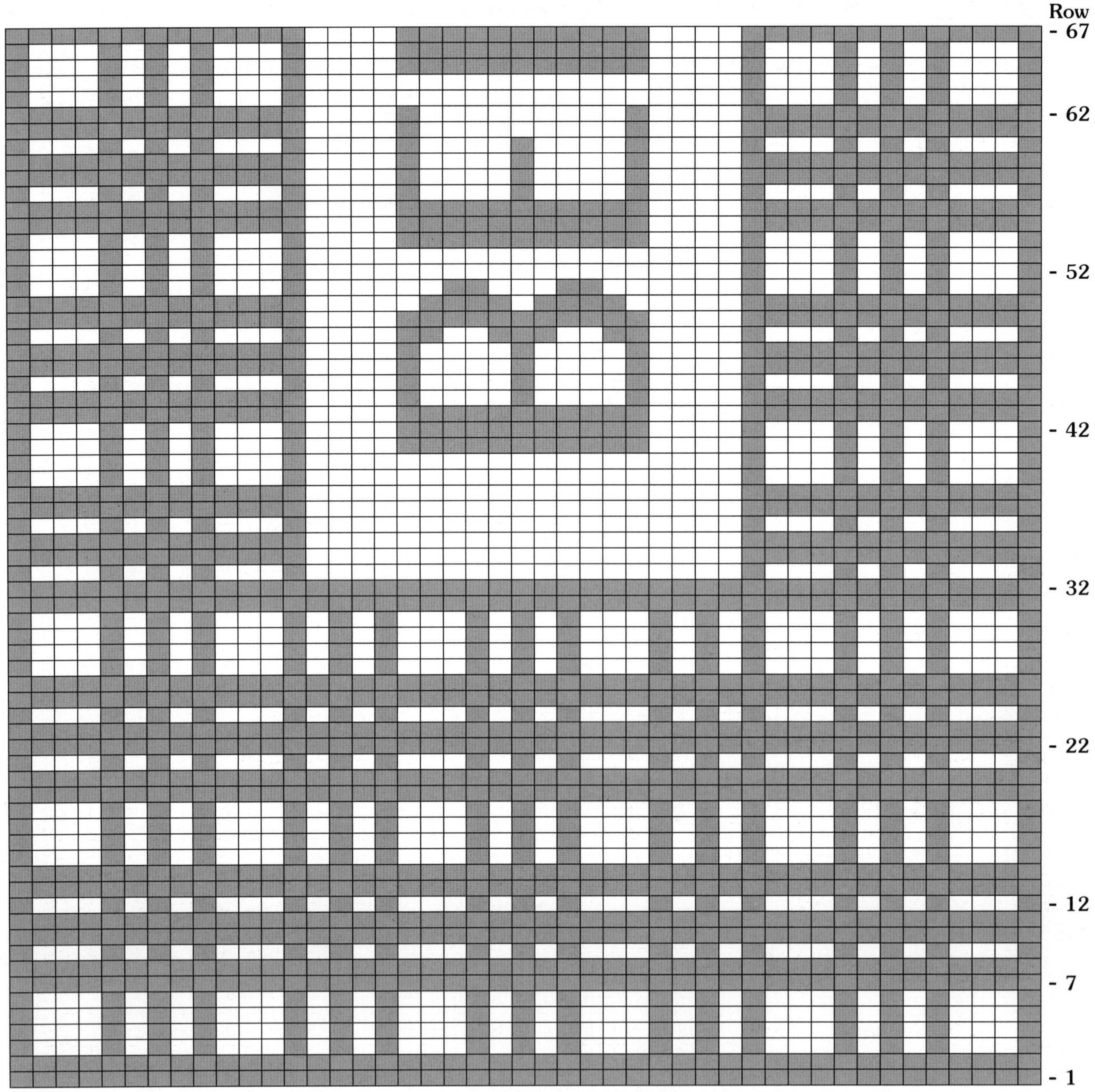

KEY

■	- Block
□	- Space

On **right** side rows, follow chart from **right** to **left**;
On **wrong** side rows, follow chart from **left** to **right**.

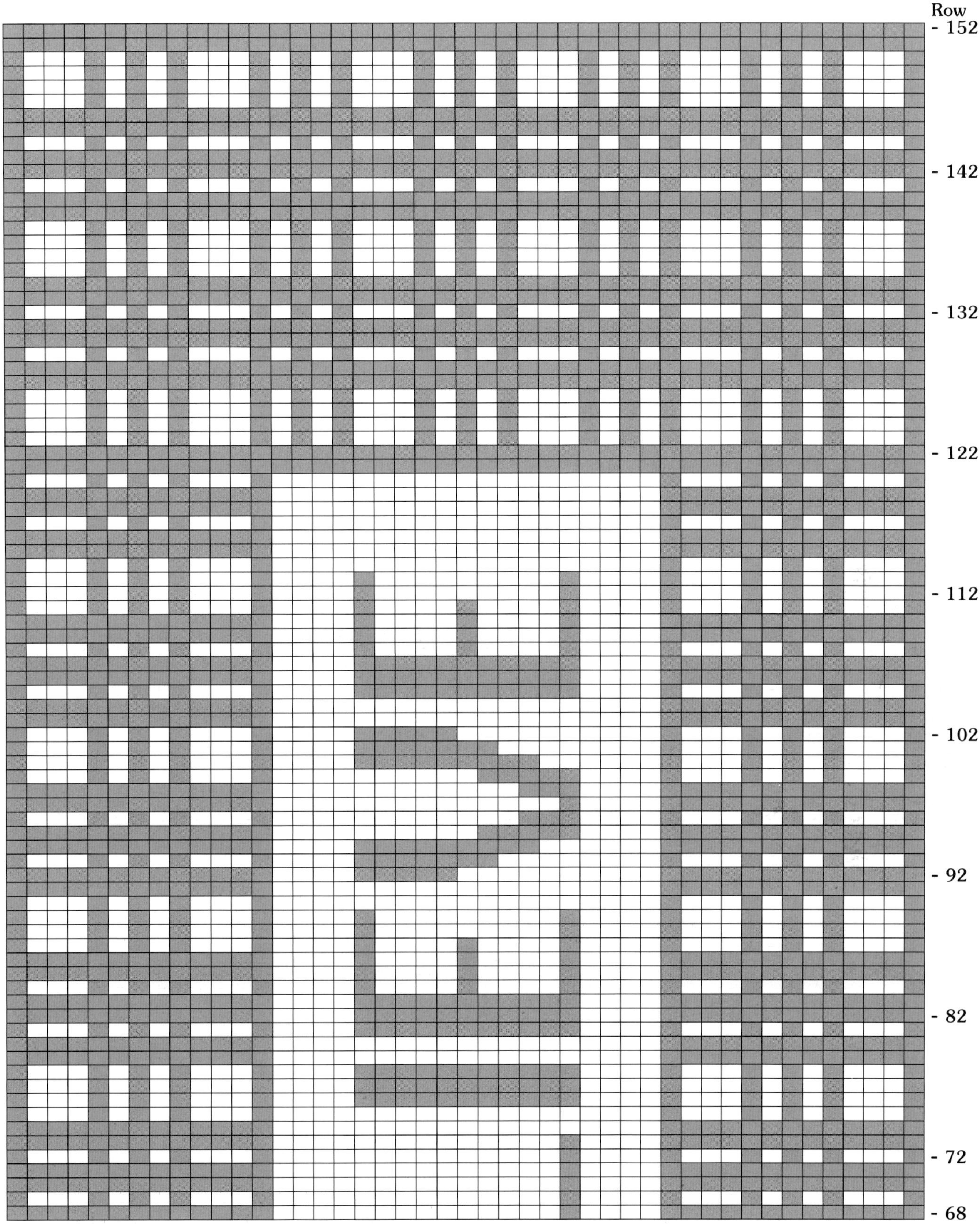
Row
- 152
- 142
- 132
- 122
- 112
- 102
- 92
- 82
- 72
- 68

Argyle *Beloved*

EASY

Finished Size:

Size 10: 35¾"w x 15"h (91 cm x 38 cm)
Size 20: 31¾"w x 13½"h (80.5 cm x 34.5 cm)
Size 30: 28½"w x 12¼"h (72.5 cm x 31 cm)

Size Note: Materials, gauge, and gauge swatch are written for cotton thread size 10, with sizes 20 and 30 in braces { }. If only one number is given, it applies to all three weights of thread.

MATERIALS

Cotton Thread
Size 10 - [400 yards (365 meters) per ball]: 3 balls
Size 20 - [400 yards (365 meters) per ball]: 3 balls
Size 30 - [500 yards (457 meters) per ball]: 2 balls
Steel crochet hook, size 6{8-10}/1.8{1.5-1.3} mm **or** size needed for gauge

GAUGE: 18{20-22} dc and 8{9-10} rows = 2" (5 cm)

Gauge Swatch: 2" (5 cm) square
Ch 20{22-24}.
Row 1: Dc in fourth ch from hook **(3 skipped chs count as first dc)** and in each ch across: 18{20-22} dc.
Rows 2 thru 8{9-10}: Ch 3 **(counts as first dc)**, turn; dc in next dc and in each dc across.
Finish off.

BASIC CHART STITCHES

BEGINNING BLOCK OVER BLOCK
Ch 3 **(counts as first dc, now and throughout)**, turn; dc in next 3 dc.
BLOCK OVER BLOCK
Dc in next 3 dc.
BLOCK OVER SPACE
2 Dc in next ch-2 sp, dc in next dc.
SPACE OVER BLOCK
Ch 2, skip next 2 dc, dc in next dc.
SPACE OVER SPACE
Ch 2, dc in next dc.

INSTRUCTIONS

Ch 138.

Row 1: Dc in fourth ch from hook **(3 skipped chs count as first dc)** and in each ch across: 136 dc.

Row 2 (Right side)**:** Work Beginning Block, work Blocks across: 45 Blocks.

Note: Loop a short piece of thread around any stitch to mark Row 2 as **right** side.

Row 3: Work Beginning Block, (work 21 Spaces, work Block) twice.

Rows 4-143: Follow Charts, pages 8 and 9.

Finish off.

See Washing and Blocking, page 35.

CHART

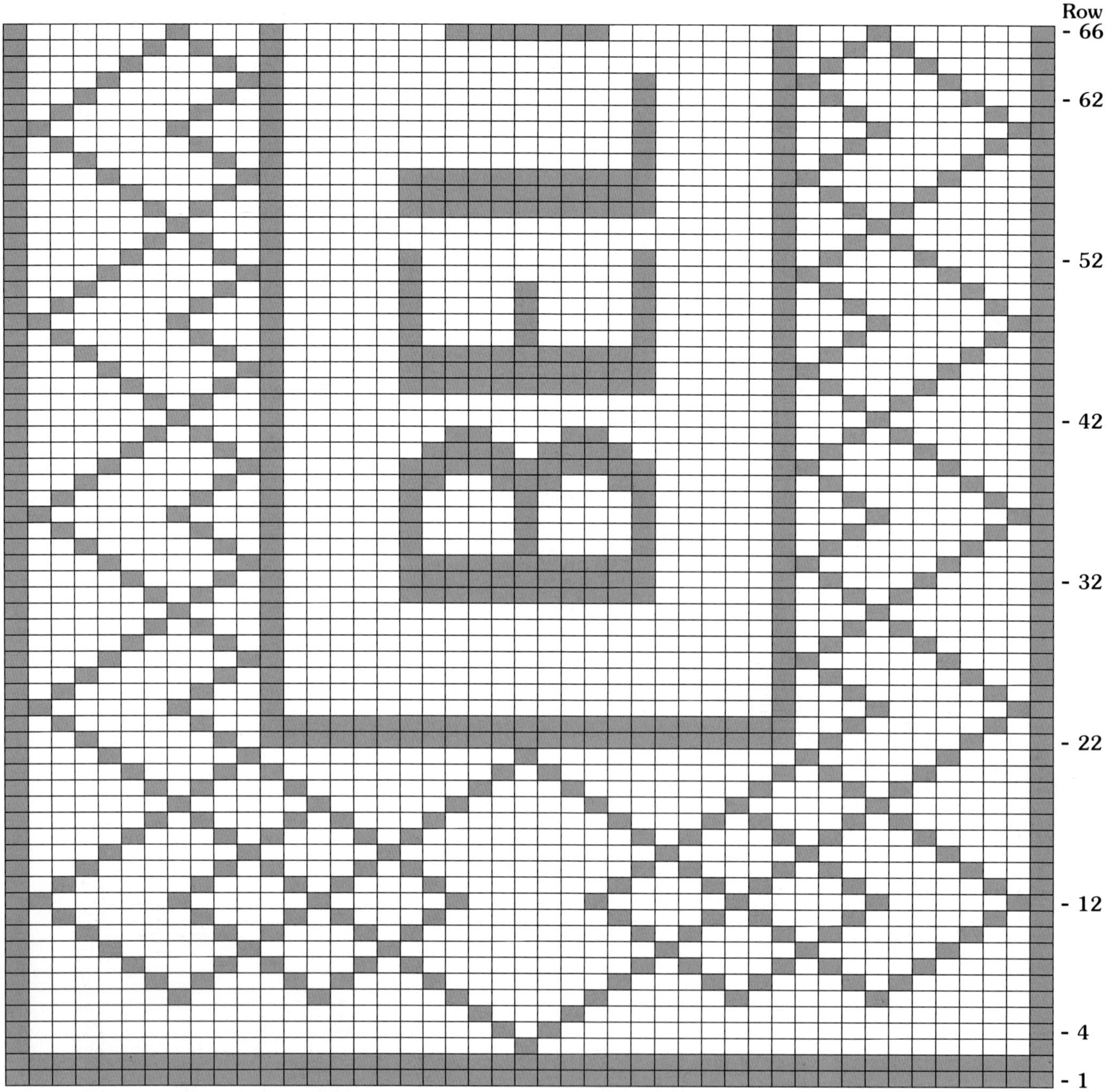

KEY

- Block
- Space

On **right** side rows, follow chart from **right** to **left**;
On **wrong** side rows, follow chart from **left** to **right**.

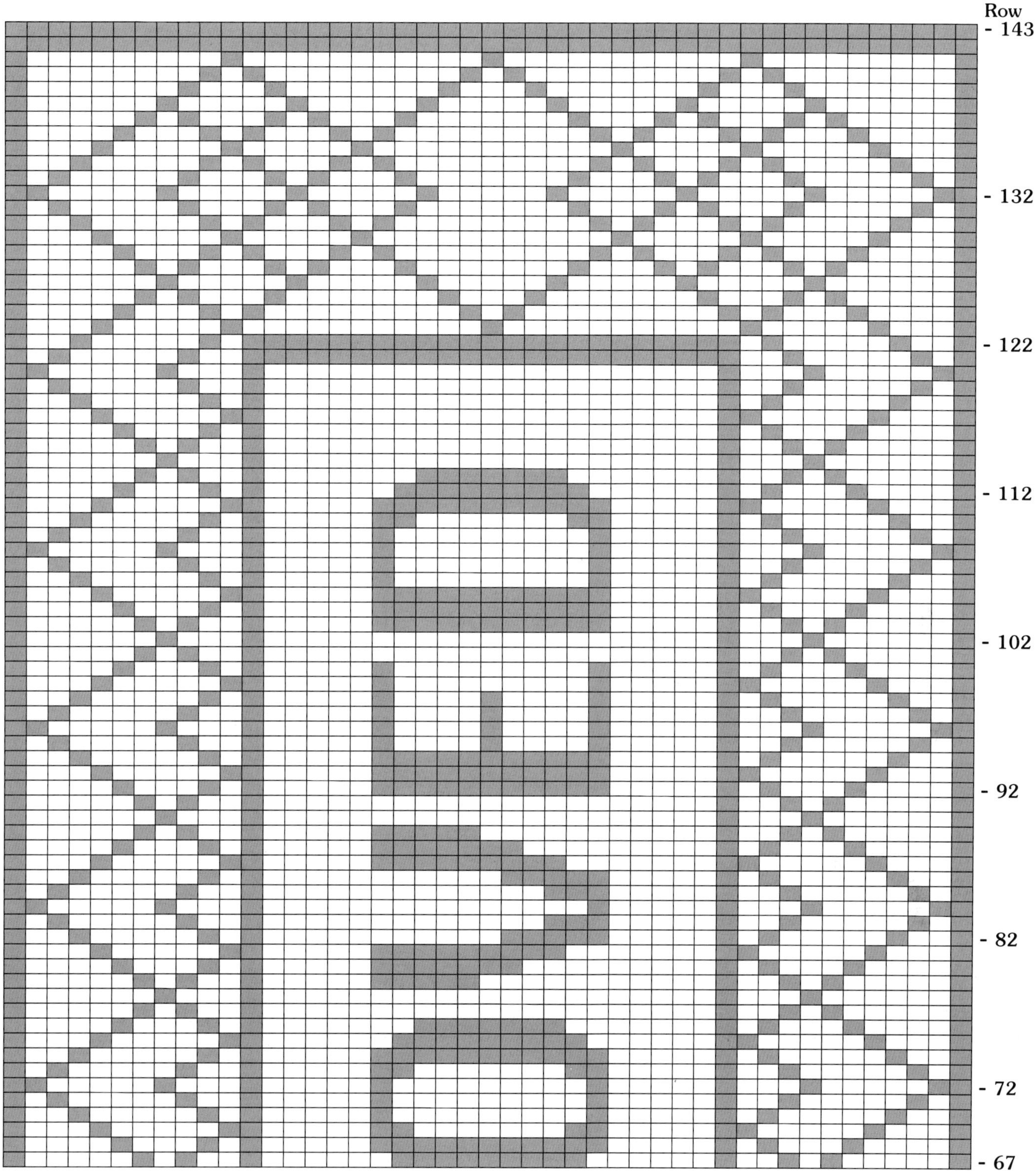
Row
- 143
- 132
- 122
- 112
- 102
- 92
- 82
- 72
- 67

Open Blocks *Cherish*

EASY

Finished Size:

Size 10: $35^3/_4$"w x 13"h (91 cm x 33 cm)
Size 20: $31^3/_4$"w x $11^3/_4$"h (80.5 cm x 30 cm)
Size 30: $28^1/_2$"w x $10^3/_4$"h (72.5 cm x 27.5 cm)

Size Note: Materials, gauge, and gauge swatch are written for cotton thread size 10, with sizes 20 and 30 in braces { }. If only one number is given, it applies to all three weights of thread.

MATERIALS

Cotton Thread
Size 10 - [400 yards (365 meters) per ball]: 2 balls
Size 20 - [400 yards (365 meters) per ball]: 2 balls
Size 30 - [500 yards (457 meters) per ball]: 2 balls
Steel crochet hook, size 6{8-10}/1.8{1.5-1.3} mm **or** size needed for gauge

GAUGE: 18{20-22} dc and 8{9-10} rows = 2" (5 cm)

Gauge Swatch: 2" (5 cm) square
Ch 20{22-24}.
Row 1: Dc in fourth ch from hook **(3 skipped chs count as first dc)** and in each ch across: 18{20-22} dc.
Rows 2 thru 8{9-10}: Ch 3 **(counts as first dc)**, turn; dc in next dc and in each dc across.
Finish off.

BASIC CHART STITCHES

BEGINNING BLOCK OVER BLOCK
Ch 3 **(counts as first dc, now and throughout)**, turn; dc in next 3 dc.
BLOCK OVER BLOCK
Dc in next 3 dc.
BLOCK OVER SPACE
2 Dc in next ch-2 sp, dc in next dc.
SPACE OVER BLOCK
Ch 2, skip next 2 dc, dc in next dc.
SPACE OVER SPACE
Ch 2, dc in next dc.

INSTRUCTIONS

Ch 120.

Row 1: Dc in fourth ch from hook **(3 skipped chs count as first dc)** and in each ch across: 118 dc.

Row 2 (Right side)**:** Work Beginning Block, work Blocks across: 39 Blocks.

Note: Loop a short piece of thread around any stitch to mark Row 2 as **right** side.

Row 3: Work Beginning Block, (work Block, work 5 Spaces) 6 times, work 2 Blocks.

Rows 4-143: Follow Charts, pages 12 and 13.

Finish off.

See Washing and Blocking, page 35.

CHART

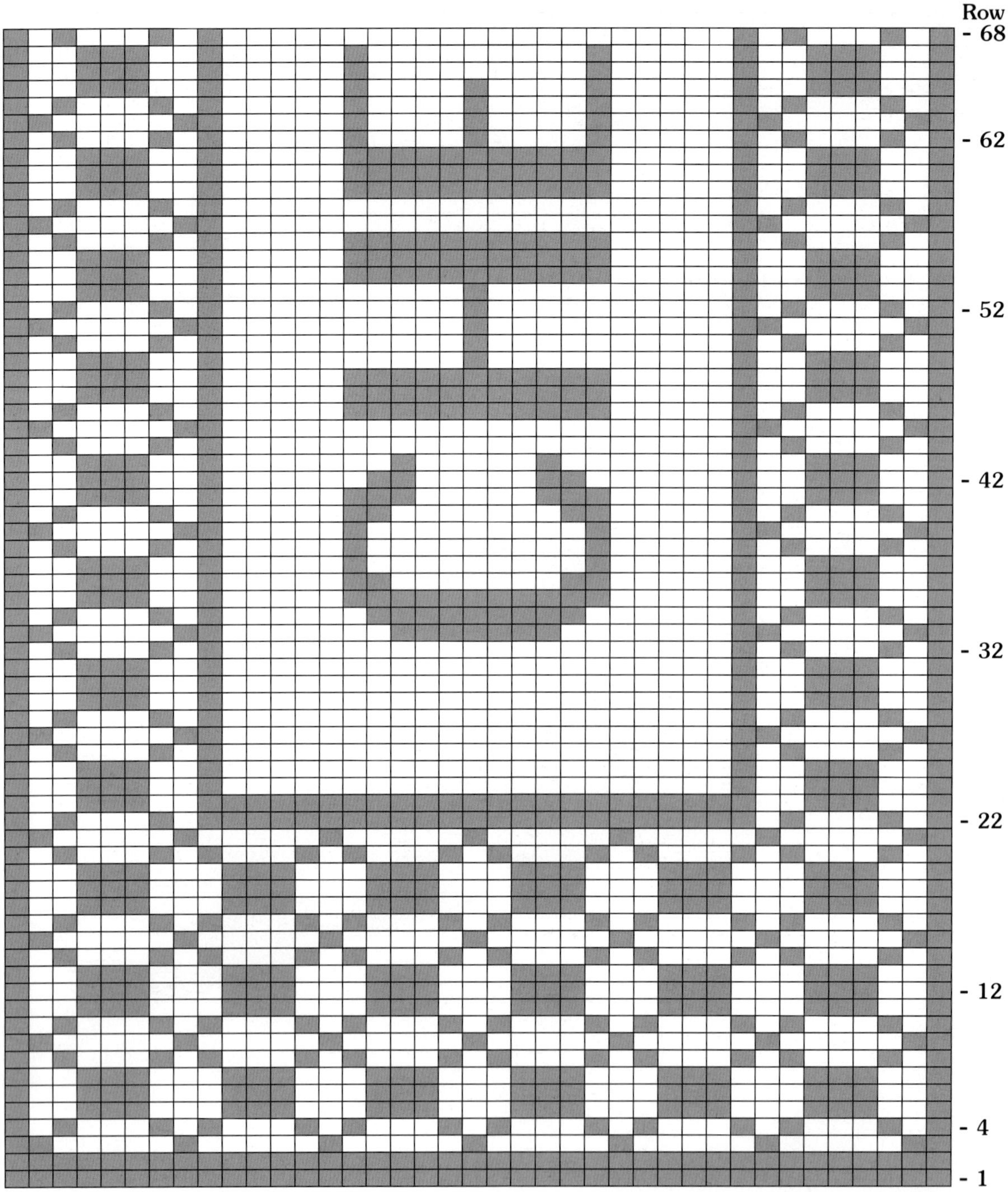

KEY

- Block
- Space

On **right** side rows, follow chart from **right** to **left**;
On **wrong** side rows, follow chart from **left** to **right**.

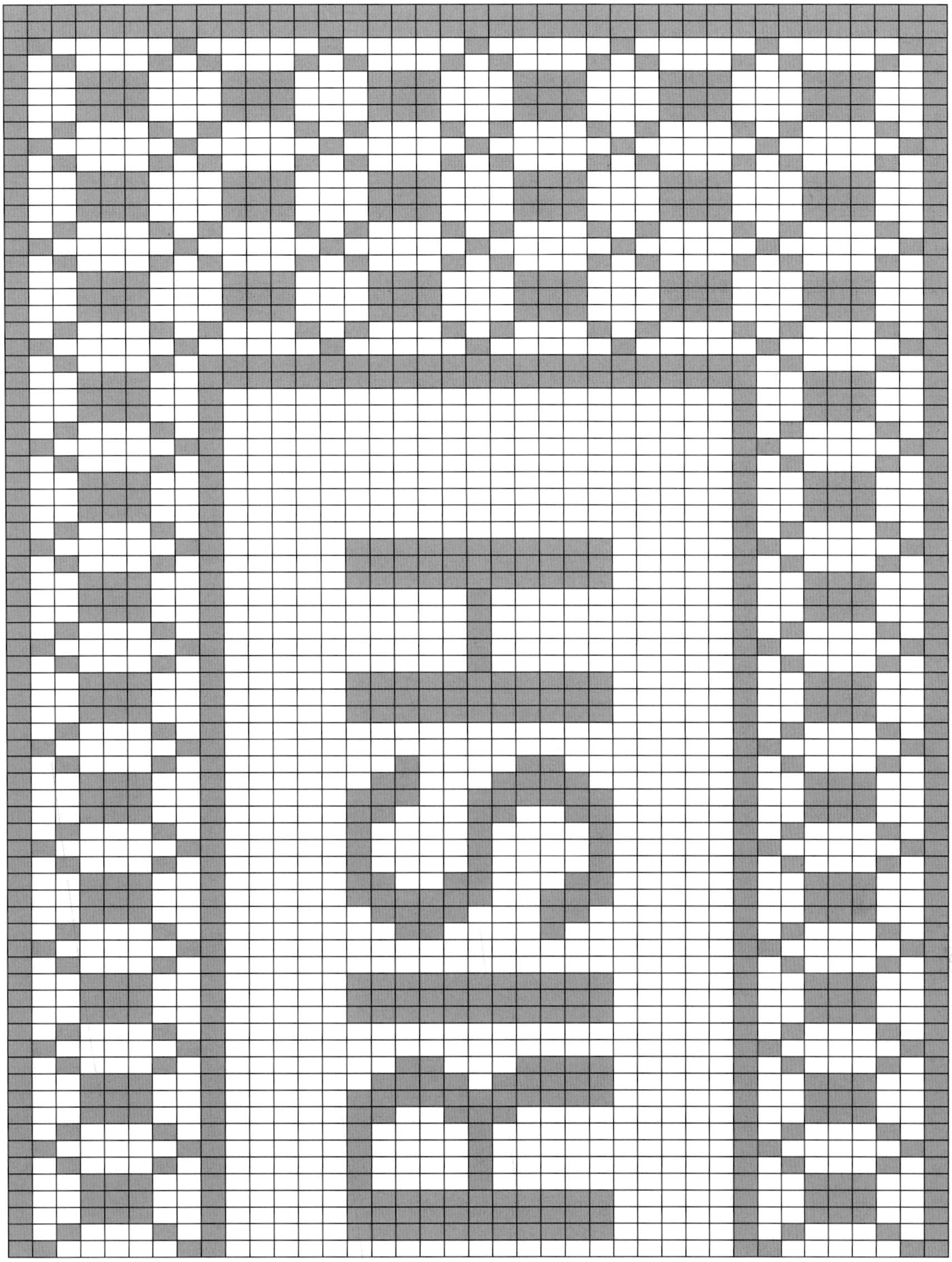
Row
- 143
- 132
- 122
- 112
- 102
- 92
- 82
- 72
- 69

Blocks Courage

EASY

Finished Size:
Size 10: 36¼"w x 14½"h (92 cm x 37 cm)
Size 20: 32¼"w x 13"h (82 cm x 33 cm)
Size 30: 29"w x 11¾"h (73.5 cm x 30 cm)

Size Note: Materials, gauge, and gauge swatch are written for cotton thread size 10, with sizes 20 and 30 in braces { }. If only one number is given, it applies to all three weights of thread.

MATERIALS
Cotton Thread
Size 10 - **[**400 yards (365 meters) per ball**]**: 3 balls
Size 20 - **[**400 yards (365 meters) per ball**]**: 3 balls
Size 30 - **[**500 yards (457 meters) per ball**]**: 2 balls
Steel crochet hook, size 6{8-10}/1.8{1.5-1.3} mm **or** size needed for gauge

GAUGE: 18{20-22} dc and 8{9-10} rows = 2" (5 cm)

Gauge Swatch: 2" (5 cm) square
Ch 20{22-24}.
Row 1: Dc in fourth ch from hook **(3 skipped chs count as first dc)** and in each ch across: 18{20-22} dc.
Rows 2 thru 8{9-10}: Ch 3 **(counts as first dc)**, turn; dc in next dc and in each dc across.
Finish off.

BASIC CHART STITCHES

BEGINNING BLOCK OVER BLOCK
Ch 3 **(counts as first dc, now and throughout)**, turn; dc in next 3 dc.
BLOCK OVER BLOCK
Dc in next 3 dc.
BLOCK OVER SPACE
2 Dc in next ch-2 sp, dc in next dc.
SPACE OVER BLOCK
Ch 2, skip next 2 dc, dc in next dc.
SPACE OVER SPACE
Ch 2, dc in next dc.

INSTRUCTIONS

Ch 132.

Row 1: Dc in fourth ch from hook **(3 skipped chs count as first dc)** and in each ch across: 130 dc.

Row 2 (Right side)**:** Work Beginning Block, work Blocks across: 43 Blocks.

Note: Loop a short piece of thread around any stitch to mark Row 2 as **right** side.

Row 3: Work Beginning Block, (work Block, work 3 Spaces) 10 times, work 2 Blocks.

Rows 4-145: Follow Charts, pages 16 and 17.

Finish off.

See Washing and Blocking, page 35.

COURAGE

CHART

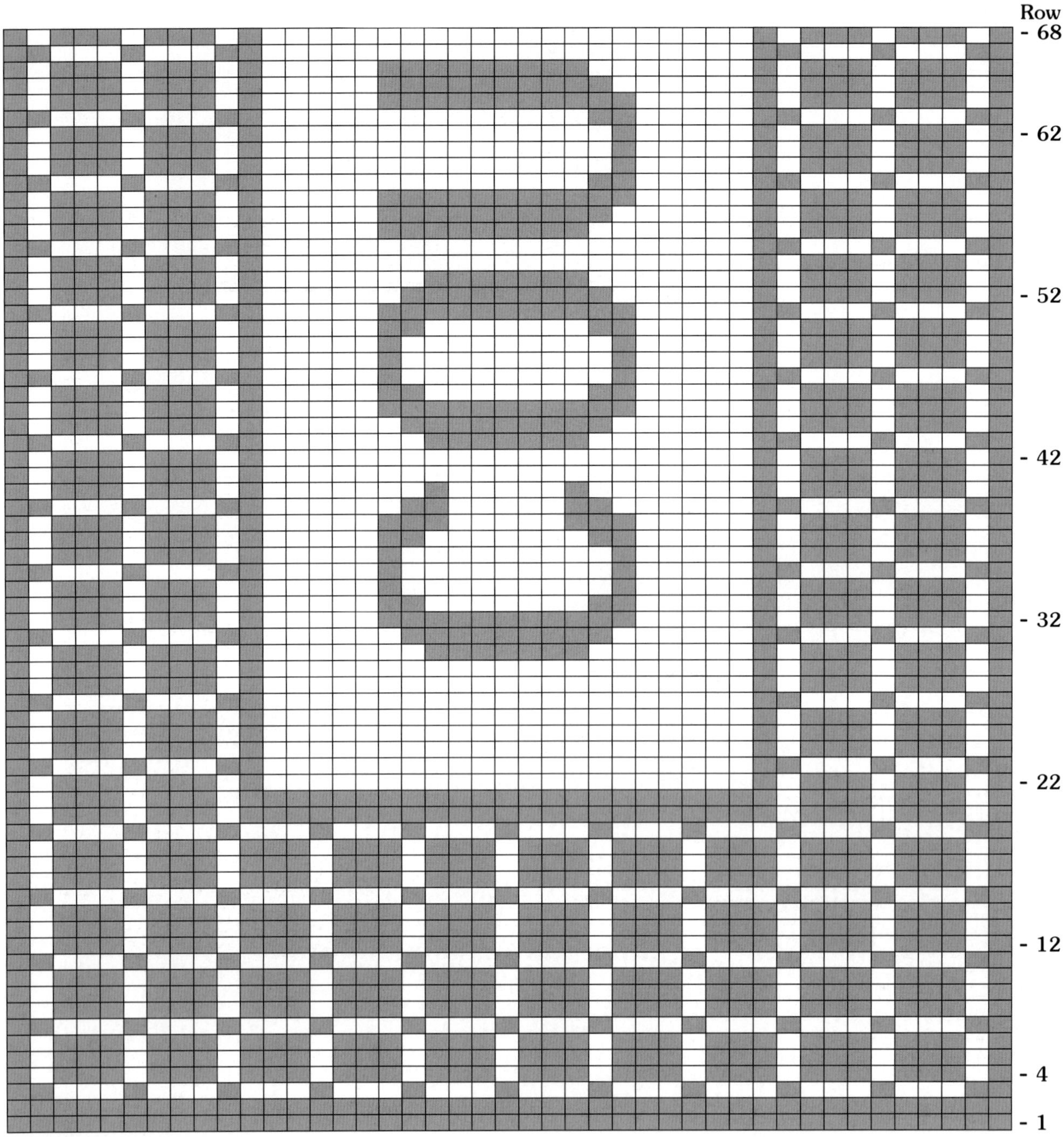

KEY

■	- Block
□	- Space

On **right** side rows, follow chart from **right** to **left**;
On **wrong** side rows, follow chart from **left** to **right**.

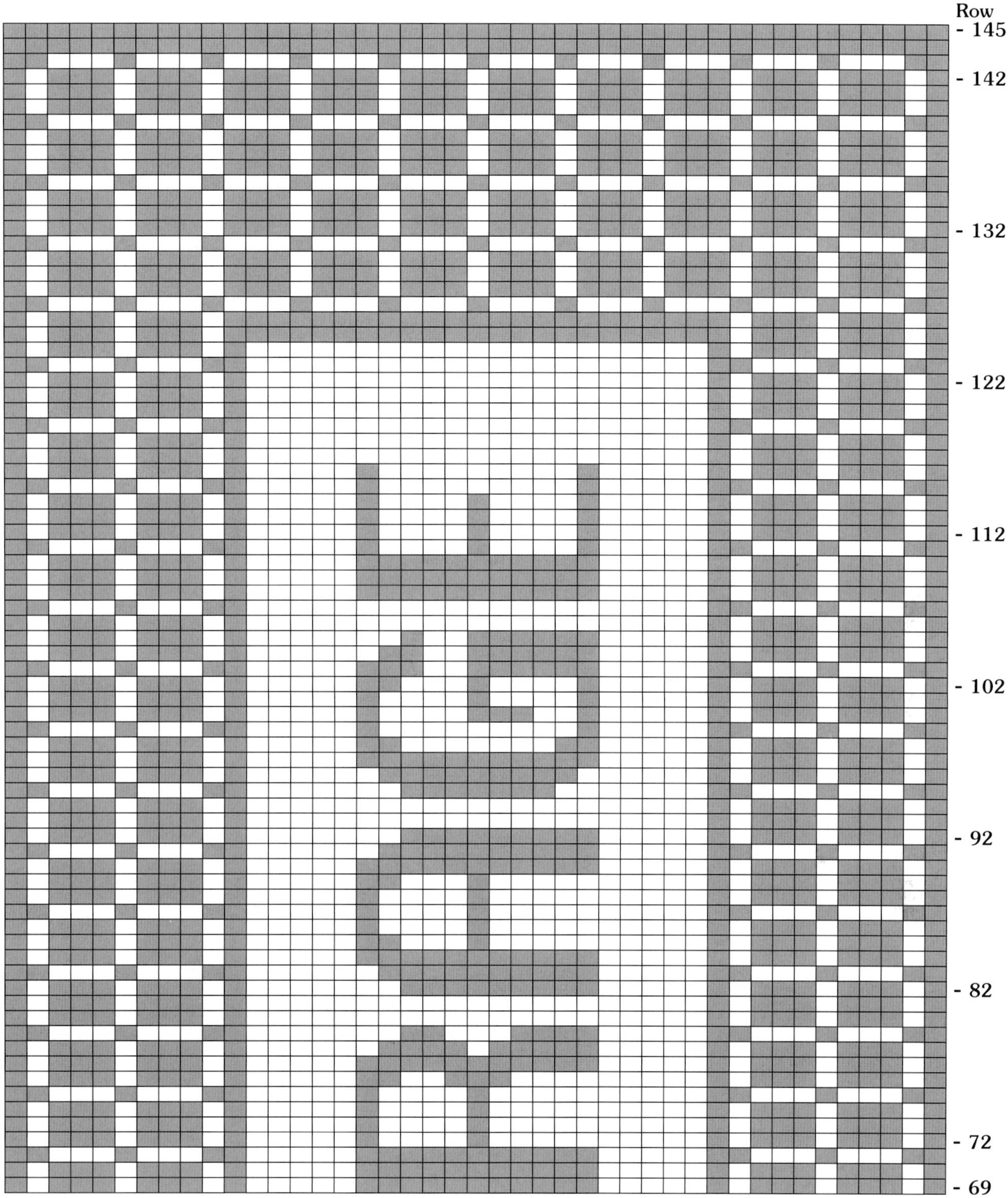
Row
- 145
- 142
- 132
- 122
- 112
- 102
- 92
- 82
- 72
- 69

Diamonds Precious

EASY

Finished Size:

Size 10: 41¼"w x 14½"h (105 cm x 37 cm)
Size 20: 36¾"w x 13"h (93.5 cm x 33 cm)
Size 30: 33"w x 11¾"h (84 cm x 30 cm)

Size Note: Materials, gauge, and gauge swatch are written for cotton thread size 10, with sizes 20 and 30 in braces { }. If only one number is given, it applies to all three weights of thread.

MATERIALS

Cotton Thread
Size 10 - [400 yards (365 meters) per ball]: 3 balls
Size 20 - [400 yards (365 meters) per ball]: 3 balls
Size 30 - [500 yards (457 meters) per ball]: 3 balls
Steel crochet hook, size 6{8-10}/1.8{1.5-1.3} mm **or** size needed for gauge

GAUGE: 18{20-22} dc and 8{9-10} rows = 2" (5 cm)

Gauge Swatch: 2" (5 cm) square
Ch 20{22-24}.
Row 1: Dc in fourth ch from hook **(3 skipped chs count as first dc)** and in each ch across: 18{20-22} dc.
Rows 2 thru 8{9-10}: Ch 3 **(counts as first dc)**, turn; dc in next dc and in each dc across. Finish off.

BASIC CHART STITCHES

BEGINNING BLOCK OVER BLOCK
Ch 3 **(counts as first dc, now and throughout)**, turn; dc in next 3 dc.
BLOCK OVER BLOCK
Dc in next 3 dc.
BLOCK OVER SPACE
2 Dc in next ch-2 sp, dc in next dc.
SPACE OVER BLOCK
Ch 2, skip next 2 dc, dc in next dc.
SPACE OVER SPACE
Ch 2, dc in next dc.

INSTRUCTIONS

Ch 132.

Row 1: Dc in fourth ch from hook **(3 skipped chs count as first dc)** and in each ch across: 130 dc.

Row 2 (Right side)**:** Work Beginning Block, work Blocks across: 43 Blocks.

Note: Loop a short piece of thread around any stitch to mark Row 2 as **right** side.

Row 3: Work Beginning Block, work 2 Blocks, (work 5 Spaces, work 3 Blocks) across.

Rows 4-165: Follow Charts, pages 20 and 21.

Finish off.

See Washing and Blocking, page 35.

CHART

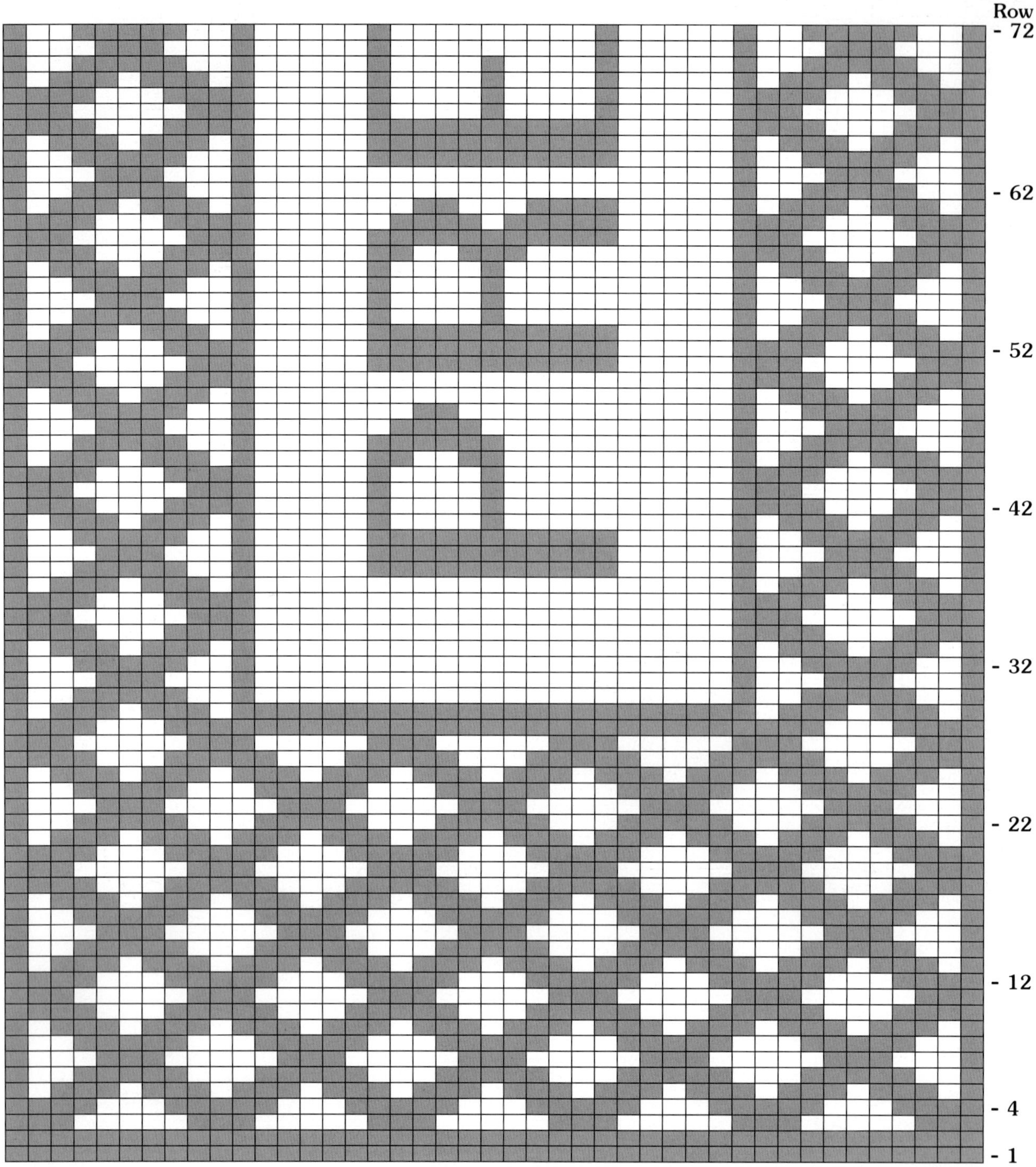

KEY

- Block
- Space

On **right** side rows, follow chart from **right** to **left**;
On **wrong** side rows, follow chart from **left** to **right**.

Row
- 165
- 162
- 152
- 142
- 132
- 122
- 112
- 102
- 92
- 82
- 73

Basket Weave *Promise*

EASY

Finished Size:
Size 10: 41"w x 15"h (104 cm x 38 cm)
Size 20: 36$^1/_2$"w x 13$^1/_2$"h (92.5 cm x 34.5 cm)
Size 30: 32$^3/_4$"w x 12$^1/_4$"h (83 cm x 31 cm)

Size Note: Materials, gauge, and gauge swatch are written for cotton thread size 10, with sizes 20 and 30 in braces { }. If only one number is given, it applies to all three weights of thread.

MATERIALS

Cotton Thread
Size 10 - [400 yards (365 meters) per ball]: 3 balls
Size 20 - [400 yards (365 meters) per ball]: 3 balls
Size 30 - [500 yards (457 meters) per ball]: 3 balls
Steel crochet hook, size 6{8-10}/1.8{1.5-1.3} mm **or** size needed for gauge

GAUGE: 18{20-22} dc and 8{9-10} rows = 2" (5 cm)

Gauge Swatch: 2" (5 cm) square
Ch 20{22-24}.
Row 1: Dc in fourth ch from hook **(3 skipped chs count as first dc)** and in each ch across: 18{20-22} dc.
Rows 2 thru 8{9-10}: Ch 3 **(counts as first dc)**, turn; dc in next dc and in each dc across. Finish off.

BASIC CHART STITCHES

BEGINNING BLOCK OVER BLOCK
Ch 3 **(counts as first dc, now and throughout)**, turn; dc in next 3 dc.
BLOCK OVER BLOCK
Dc in next 3 dc.
BLOCK OVER SPACE
2 Dc in next ch-2 sp, dc in next dc.
SPACE OVER BLOCK
Ch 2, skip next 2 dc, dc in next dc.
SPACE OVER SPACE
Ch 2, dc in next dc.

INSTRUCTIONS

Ch 138.

Row 1: Dc in fourth ch from hook **(3 skipped chs count as first dc)** and in each ch across: 136 dc.

Row 2 (Right side)**:** Work Beginning Block, work Blocks across: 45 Blocks.

Note: Loop a short piece of thread around any stitch to mark Row 2 as **right** side.

Rows 3-6: Work Beginning Block, work 3 Spaces, work Block, ★ (work Space, work Block) twice, work 3 Spaces, work Block; repeat from ★ across.

Rows 7-164: Follow Charts, pages 24 and 25.

Finish off.

See Washing and Blocking, page 35.

CHART

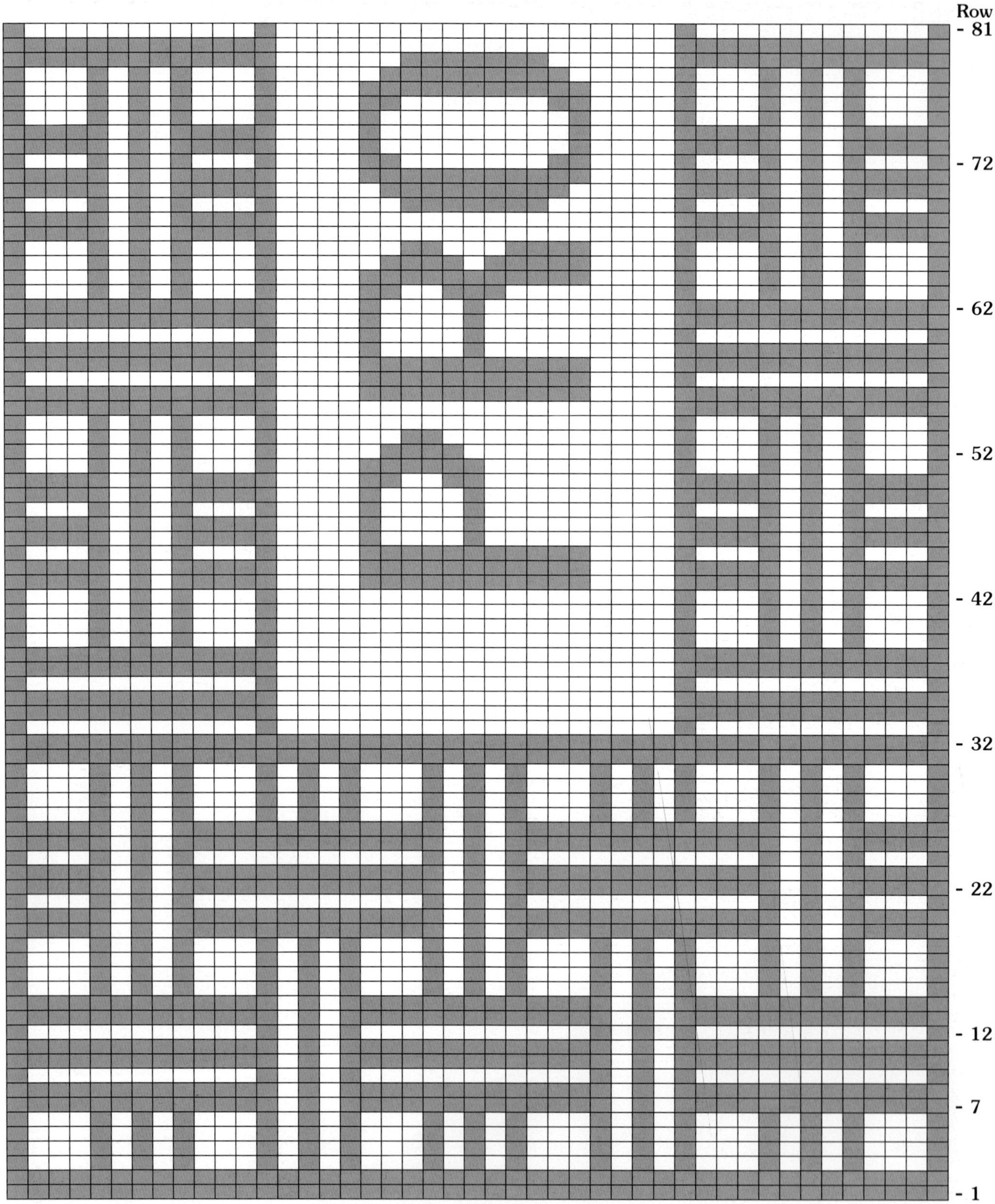

KEY

- Block
- Space

On **right** side rows, follow chart from **right** to **left**;
On **wrong** side rows, follow chart from **left** to **right**.

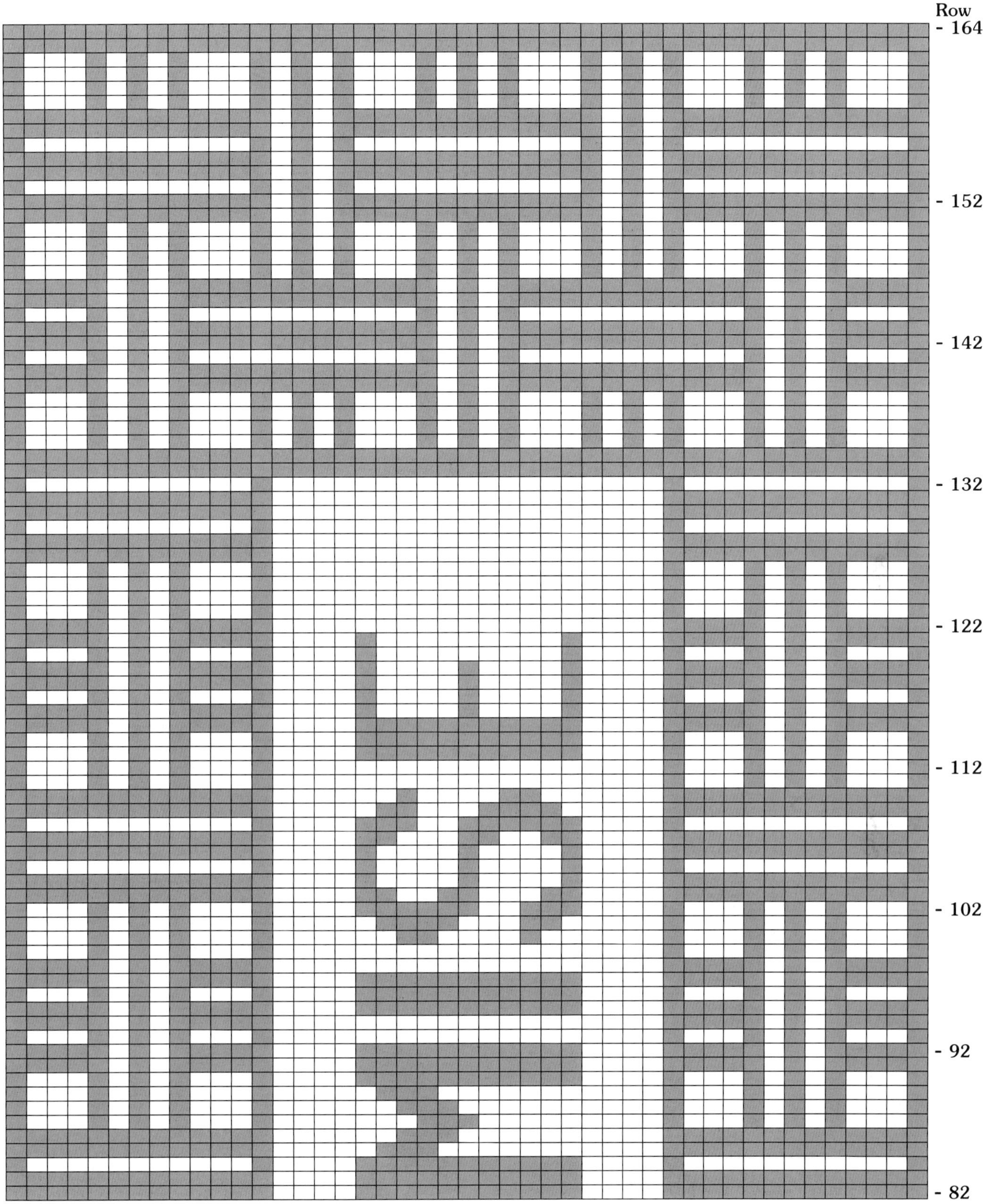
Row
- 164
- 152
- 142
- 132
- 122
- 112
- 102
- 92
- 82

Brick Work *Strength*

EASY

Finished Size:

Size 10: $42^1/_2$"w x 15"h (108 cm x 38 cm)
Size 20: $37^3/_4$"w x $13^1/_2$"h (96 cm x 34.5 cm)
Size 30: 34"w x $12^1/_4$"h (86.5 cm x 31 cm)

Size Note: Materials, gauge, and gauge swatch are written for cotton thread size 10, with sizes 20 and 30 in braces { }. If only one number is given, it applies to all three weights of thread.

MATERIALS

Cotton Thread
Size 10 - [400 yards (365 meters) per ball]:
3 balls
Size 20 - [400 yards (365 meters) per ball]:
3 balls
Size 30 - [500 yards (457 meters) per ball]:
3 balls
Steel crochet hook,
size 6{8-10}/1.8{1.5-1.3} mm **or**
size needed for gauge

GAUGE: 18{20-22} dc and
8{9-10} rows = 2" (5 cm)

Gauge Swatch: 2" (5 cm) square
Ch 20{22-24}.
Row 1: Dc in fourth ch from hook **(3 skipped chs count as first dc)** and in each ch across: 18{20-22} dc.
Rows 2 thru 8{9-10}: Ch 3 **(counts as first dc)**, turn; dc in next dc and in each dc across.
Finish off.

BASIC CHART STITCHES

BEGINNING BLOCK OVER BLOCK
Ch 3 **(counts as first dc, now and throughout)**, turn; dc in next 3 dc.
BLOCK OVER BLOCK
Dc in next 3 dc.
BLOCK OVER SPACE
2 Dc in next ch-2 sp, dc in next dc.
SPACE OVER BLOCK
Ch 2, skip next 2 dc, dc in next dc.
SPACE OVER SPACE
Ch 2, dc in next dc.

INSTRUCTIONS

Ch 138.

Row 1: Dc in fourth ch from hook **(3 skipped chs count as first dc)** and in each ch across: 136 dc.

Row 2 (Right side)**:** Work Beginning Block, work Blocks across: 45 Blocks.

Note: Loop a short piece of thread around any stitch to mark Row 2 as **right** side.

Rows 3-6: Work Beginning Block, (work 3 Spaces, work Block) across.

Rows 7-170: Follow Charts, pages 28 and 29.

Finish off.

See Washing and Blocking, page 35.

CHART

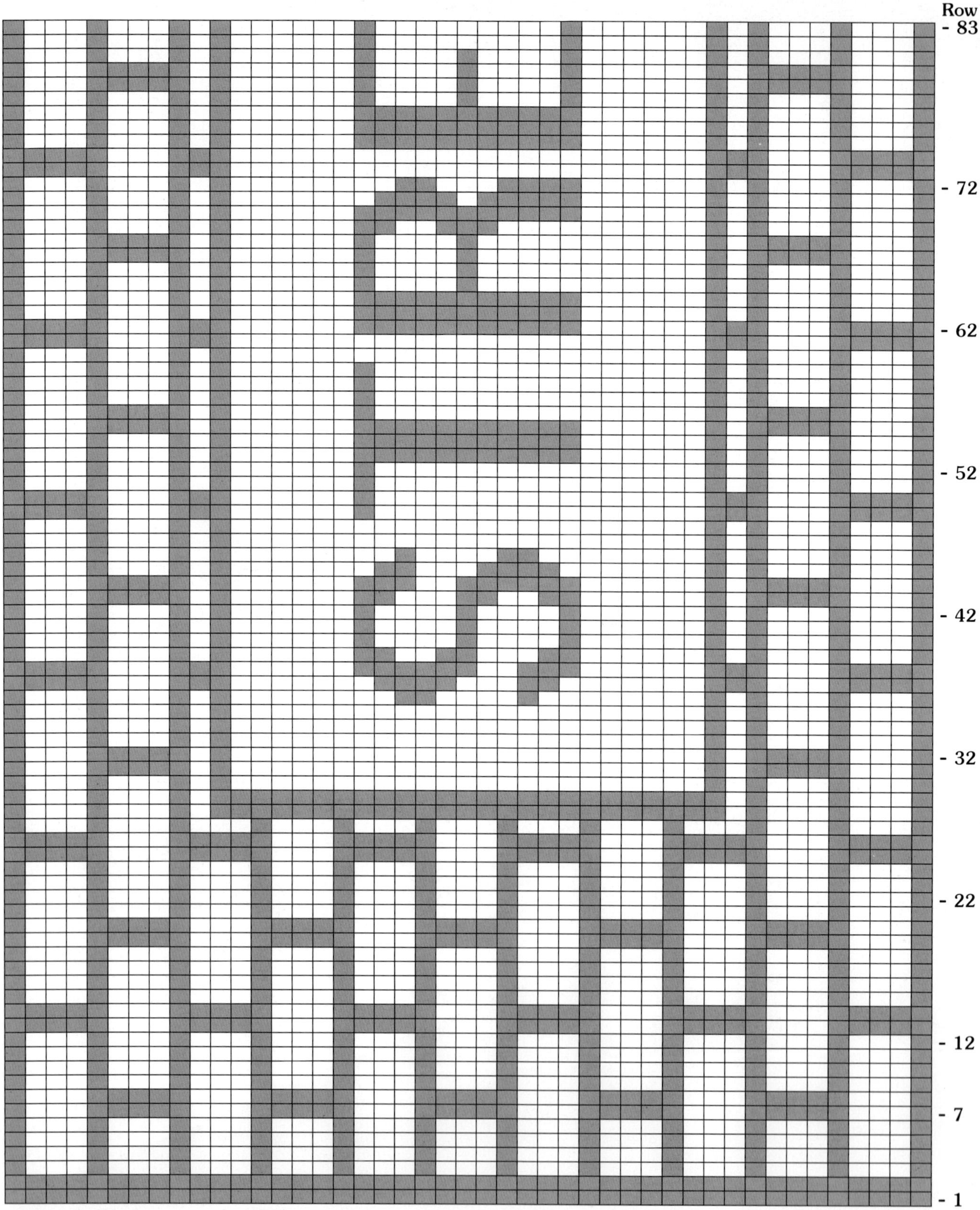

KEY

- Block
- Space

On **right** side rows, follow chart from **right** to **left**;
On **wrong** side rows, follow chart from **left** to **right**.

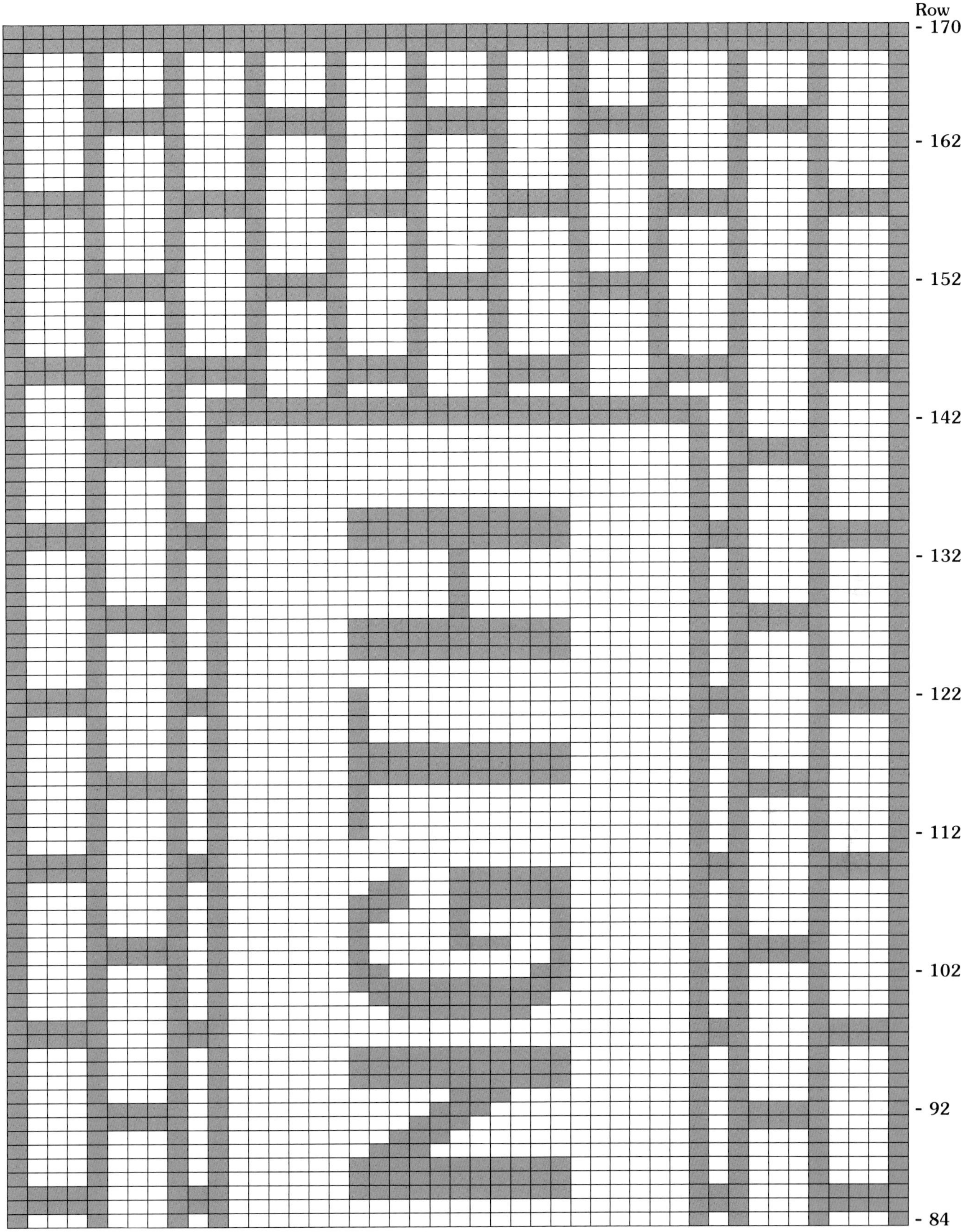
Row
170
162
152
142
132
122
112
102
92
84

Greek Key *Welcome*

EASY

Finished Size:

Size 10: 35¾"w x 15"h (91 cm x 38 cm)
Size 20: 31¾"w x 13½"h (80.5 cm x 34.5 cm)
Size 30: 28½"w x 12¼"h (72.5 cm x 31 cm)

Size Note: Materials, gauge, and gauge swatch are written for cotton thread size 10, with sizes 20 and 30 in braces { }. If only one number is given, it applies to all three weights of thread.

MATERIALS

Cotton Thread
Size 10 - [400 yards (365 meters) per ball]:
3 balls
Size 20 - [400 yards (365 meters) per ball]:
3 balls
Size 30 - [500 yards (457 meters) per ball]:
2 balls
Steel crochet hook,
size 6{8-10}/1.8{1.5-1.3} mm **or**
size needed for gauge

GAUGE: 18{20-22} dc and
8{9-10} rows = 2" (5 cm)

Gauge Swatch: 2" (5 cm) square
Ch 20{22-24}.
Row 1: Dc in fourth ch from hook **(3 skipped chs count as first dc)** and in each ch across: 18{20-22} dc.
Rows 2 thru 8{9-10}: Ch 3 **(counts as first dc)**, turn; dc in next dc and in each dc across.
Finish off.

BASIC CHART STITCHES

BEGINNING BLOCK OVER BLOCK
Ch 3 **(counts as first dc, now and throughout)**, turn; dc in next 3 dc.
BLOCK OVER BLOCK
Dc in next 3 dc.
BLOCK OVER SPACE
2 Dc in next ch-2 sp, dc in next dc.
SPACE OVER BLOCK
Ch 2, skip next 2 dc, dc in next dc.
SPACE OVER SPACE
Ch 2, dc in next dc.

INSTRUCTIONS

Ch 138.

Row 1: Dc in fourth ch from hook **(3 skipped chs count as first dc)** and in each ch across: 136 dc.

Row 2 (Right side)**:** Work Beginning Block, work Blocks across: 45 Blocks.

Note: Loop a short piece of thread around any stitch to mark Row 2 as **right** side.

Row 3: Work Beginning Block, work 43 Spaces, work Block.

Rows 4-143: Follow Charts, pages 32 and 33.

Finish off.

See Washing and Blocking, page 35.

WELCOME

CHART

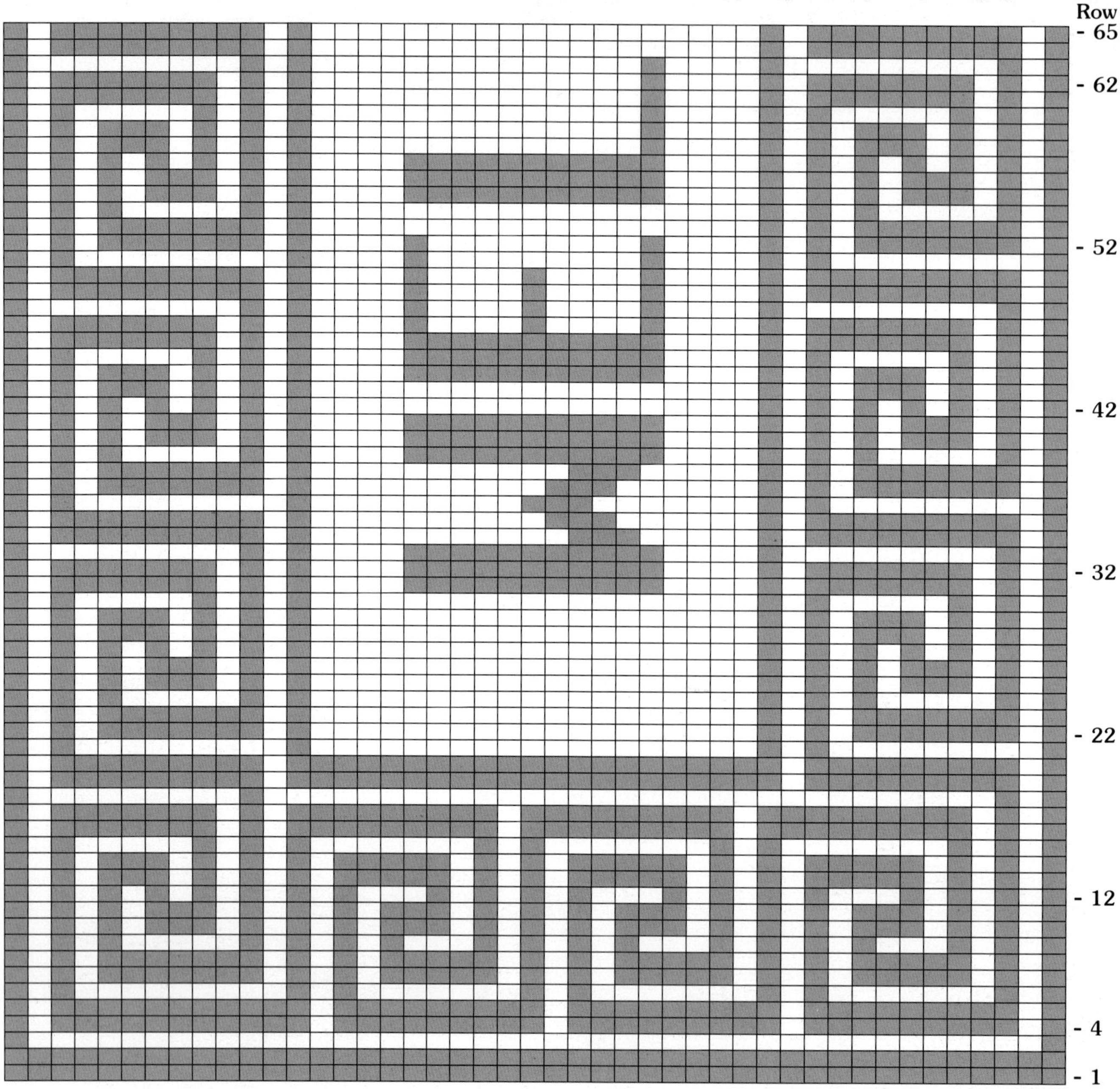

KEY

- Block
- Space

On **right** side rows, follow chart from **right** to **left**;
On **wrong** side rows, follow chart from **left** to **right**.

Row
- 143
- 132
- 122
- 112
- 102
- 92
- 82
- 72
- 66

General Instructions

ABBREVIATIONS

ch(s) chain(s)
cm centimeters
dc double crochet(s)
mm millimeters
sp(s) space(s)

★ — work instructions following ★ as many **more** times as indicated in addition to the first time.
( ) or [ ] — work enclosed instructions **as many** times as specified by the number immediately following **or** contains explanatory remarks.
colon (:)— the number(s) given after a colon at the end of a row or round denote(s) the number of stitches you should have on that row or round.

GAUGE

Exact gauge is **essential** for proper size. Before beginning your project, make the sample swatch given in the individual instructions in the thread and hook specified. After completing the swatch, measure it, counting your stitches and rows carefully. If your swatch is larger or smaller than specified, **make another, changing hook size to get the correct gauge**. Keep trying until you find the size hook that will give you the specified gauge.

CROCHET TERMINOLOGY		
UNITED STATES		**INTERNATIONAL**
slip stitch (slip st)	=	single crochet (sc)
single crochet (sc)	=	double crochet (dc)
half double crochet (hdc)	=	half treble crochet (htr)
double crochet (dc)	=	treble crochet (tr)
treble crochet (tr)	=	double treble crochet (dtr)
double treble crochet (dtr)	=	triple treble crochet (ttr)
triple treble crochet (tr tr)	=	quadruple treble crochet (qtr)
skip	=	miss

STEEL CROCHET HOOKS																
U.S.	00	0	1	2	3	4	5	6	7	8	9	10	11	12	13	14
Metric - mm	3.5	3.25	2.75	2.25	2.1	2	1.9	1.8	1.65	1.5	1.4	1.3	1.1	1	.85	.75

BEGINNER	Projects for first-time crocheters using basic stitches. Minimal shaping.
EASY	Projects using yarn with basic stitches, repetitive stitch patterns, simple color changes, and simple shaping and finishing.
INTERMEDIATE	Projects using a variety of techniques, such as basic lace patterns or color patterns, mid-level shaping and finishing.
EXPERIENCED	Projects with intricate stitch patterns, techniques and dimension, such as non-repeating patterns, multi-color techniques, fine threads, small hooks, detailed shaping and refined finishing.

THREAD

The photographed items were made using bedspread weight cotton thread (size 10). Any of the following brands may be used with good results:

Aunt Lydia's® Classic Crochet
Coats Opera
DMC® Baroque
DMC® Cebelia
DMC® Cordonnet Special
DMC® Traditions
Grandma's Best
J & P Coats® Royale™
Lily® Antique
South Maid®

WASHING AND BLOCKING

For a more professional look, pieces should be washed and blocked. Using a mild detergent and warm water and being careful not to rub, twist, or wring, gently squeeze suds through the piece. Rinse several times in cool, clear water. Roll piece in a clean terry towel and gently press out the excess moisture. Lay piece on a flat surface and shape to proper size; where needed, pin in place using rust-proof pins. Allow to dry **completely**.

Thread Information

Each piece in this leaflet was made using Aunt Lydia's® Classic Crochet Cotton Thread (size 10), #1 White. Any brand of cotton thread may be used. Remember, to arrive at the finished size, it is the GAUGE/TENSION that is important, not the brand of thread.

Production Team: Writer/Technical Editor - Linda Luder; Editorial Writer - Susan McManus Johnson; Senior Graphic Artist - Lora Puls; Graphic Artist - Amy Gerke; Photo Stylist - Angela Alexander; and Photographer - Ken West.

Your opinion matters!

PLEASE SHARE
your comments and suggestions at
www.facebook.com/Official.LeisureArts

At Leisure Arts, we're excited about bringing you the most complete, easy-to-follow instructions. Let us know how we can make your creative experiences more fun, more rewarding--and yes, even easier!